FROM
ISOLATION
TO POPULATION

Eric Devon Jefferson, Jr.

From Isolation to Population © 2025 by Eric Devon Jefferson, Jr. All Rights Reserved.

All rights reserved. No part of this book may be reproduced in any form or by any electronic or mechanical means, including information storage and retrieval systems, without permission in writing from the author. The only exception is by a reviewer, who may quote short excerpts in a review.

"Scripture quotations are from the ESV® Bible (The Holy Bible, English Standard Version®), © 2001 by Crossway, a publishing ministry of Good News Publishers. ESV Text Edition: 2025. The ESV text may not be quoted in any publication made available to the public by a Creative Commons license. The ESV may not be translated in whole or in part into any other language. Used by permission. All rights reserved.

Printed in the United States of America
First Printing: October 2025
The Scribe Tribe Publishing Group

ISBN-978-1-958436-50-9 (print)
ISBN – 978-1-958436-51-6 (ebook)

Dedication

This book is dedicated to every soul who has ever felt isolated, trapped, overlooked, misunderstood, abandoned, or broken. To those who have cried silent tears, fought unseen battles, and wrestled with invisible chains—you are not forgotten.

To the ones who are currently incarcerated and feel like no one remembers you—this is for you. To the veterans and soldiers who've been placed in situations you never imagined you'd face—you are seen. To those battling deep depression and thinking life is over—I'm here to tell you, it's not.

This book is a reminder that being isolated does not mean being abandoned by God. It means being set apart with Him. Sometimes, isolation is the place where transformation begins. May these pages bring you hope, healing, and the truth that God still has a plan for your life.

Also, I dedicate this book to all those who prayed for me and continued to believe God for His purpose over my life, even when it was hard for me to see it. Thank you for your faithful prayers.

Acknowledgments

First and foremost, I thank my Lord and Savior, Jesus Christ, whose mercy preserved me, whose grace restored me, and whose love redeemed me from the ashes.

To my faithful mother, Ida Martin, you prayed for me when I didn't even realize I needed it. Your love and prayers covered me. To my grandmothers, Dorothy Boyd and Mary Jefferson, you showed me what strength, grace, and unwavering faith looks like. To my father, Eric Devon Jefferson Sr., my stepmother, Felicia Jefferson, and my stepfather, Anthony Martin Sr., thank you for the roles you played in God's divine plan for my life.

To Myla, you are my answered prayer. Your loyalty and love reflect the heart of God to me every day.

To my children, you are the legacy of God's redemption.

To my siblings, family, and every friend who remained when others walked away, thank you.

To Brothers in the Word—Pastor Tim, Pastor Sam, and Brother Dana—you sharpened me, challenged me, and supported me. You helped me find my voice again.

To the Veterans Treatment Court Program, thank you for being a vessel of God's mercy. Without God allowing the establishment of this program, I don't know where I would be today. God showed me that even in the court system, His presence is there; He utilized the justice and decisional abilities of Judge John Fitzgerald Lyke, Jr. for the positive impact over my life and the lives of many people

And to every soul who whispered a prayer on my behalf, you are part of the miracle God performed in my life. Thank you all!

Table of Contents

The Story Behind the Title... 1
Day 1: The Seed Was Planted... 3
Day 2: Jonah's Journey and Mine.. 5
Day 3: Growing in the Storm... 9
Day 4: God Is My Defender.. 11
Day 5: Church Is Not Walls—Church Is the Body.................. 13
Day 6: Praying in Elkhart Jail... 17
Day 7: The Power of Fasting.. 19
Day 8: Brothers in the Word.. 21
Day 9: Free in the Spirit, Though Bound in Chains................ 23
Day 10: God's Mercy Speaks Louder Than Man's Judgment......... 25
Day 11: Feeding on the Right Things.................................. 29
Day 12: Dreams and Deliverance...................................... 33
Day 13: Stay Low to Stay Holy... 37
Day 14: A Second Chance to Love.................................... 39
Day 15: Myla Stands in the Storm
Day 16: Healed from False Accusations............................. 43
Day 17: My Father's Grace and Forgiveness........................ 47
Day 18: No Life Without God's Presence............................ 49
Day 19: Rooted in the Word Through Trials........................ 51
Day 20: Taste and See That the Lord Is Good...................... 53

Day 21: Freedom in Surrender...................................55

Day 22: When God Closed the Door............................57

Day 23: Victory Belongs to Obedience..........................59

Day 24: Your Weakness Is God's Opportunity.....................61

Day 25: Guard Your Heart in the Fire 63

Day 26: God is Still Writing My Story 65

Day 27: Purpose Over Popularity 67

Day 28: The Weight of Glory...................................69

Day 29: Your Story Has Power..................................71

Day 30: Isolation Was Preparation 73

Day 31: From Isolation to Population 75

How to Unlock the Promises of God............................79

Preview of **Soldier to Son** *83*

About the Author 85

The Story Behind the Title

My story doesn't begin in a jail cell. It begins on the South Side of Chicago, where life wasn't always easy, especially for someone trying to live for God. I grew up attending Apostolic Faith Church under Bishop Dr. Horace E. Smith. That was where the foundation of faith was laid in me.

Even before that, my mother and grandmother were steady examples of prayer. They didn't just tell me about God—they showed me what it meant to seek Him. I remember watching them pray and listening as they encouraged me to memorize Scripture. At that age, I didn't fully understand why they wanted me to store those verses in my heart. To me, it felt like just words to remember, but what I didn't realize was that those very words would become my lifeline in the years to come.

As I grew older, life took me through many valleys. In the military, I faced my first breaking point, where I discovered that the Word of God is not just ink on paper—it's alive. Later, I walked through seasons of debris, jail, and even prison. I also went through a divorce right before I found myself on house arrest. That season left me feeling like everything was falling apart—family, freedom, and identity all at once. And yet in every place, God revealed His Word to me in a fresh way. Time and again, He kept me, covered me, and reminded me that He had never left.

I can't take credit for surviving those moments. It wasn't my strength or my wisdom that carried me through. Looking back, I see clearly it was God's hand the whole time. Just as Psalm 91 promises, *"For He will command His angels concerning you to guard you in all your ways."*

And even before I took my first breath, His plan was already written: *"For He chose us in Him before the foundation of the world, that we should be holy and blameless before Him. In love He predestined us for adoption to Himself as sons through Jesus Christ, according to the purpose of His will"* (Ephesians 1:4–5).

This devotional is my story—but more than that, it's God's story. It's about His faithfulness, His mercy, and His power to redeem. My hope is that as you read, you don't just see me—you see the God who never left me, the God who never fails, and the God who is able to do the same for you.

DAY 1

The Seed Was Planted

Psalm 46:1 – God is our refuge and strength, a very present help in trouble.

Colossians 3:23-24 – And whatsoever ye do, do it heartily, as to the Lord, and not unto men; Knowing that of the Lord ye shall receive the reward of the inheritance: for ye serve the Lord Christ.

I grew up on the south side of Chicago, where life wasn't easy, especially if you wanted to live like Jesus. I attended Apostolic Faith Church under Bishop Dr. Horace E. Smith. It was during this season of my life when the seed of the Word of God was planted in me.

It was tough growing up in an environment surrounded by crime, pressure, and temptation. But somehow, even back then, God was preserving me. I didn't understand the fullness of it yet, but that seed was real. And even when I would drift later in life, that seed never died.

Looking back, I realize the Word never left me. It was dormant and unseen until God was ready to bring it to life. When I found myself in isolation, it wasn't new words that saved me; it was the seed that had already been planted years ago. That seed was waiting on the right conditions to sprout, and in my lowest place, it broke through.

Scripture Focus

Isaiah 55:11 - So shall my word be that goes out from my mouth; it shall not return to me empty, but it shall accomplish that which I purpose, and shall succeed in the thing for which I sent it.

Reflection

You may not feel like much is happening in your life, but if the Word has been planted in you, God is working. Seeds grow in silence. Don't judge your potential by your current position. What's buried will bloom in due season.

Questions

- Can you remember a moment when the Word of God was first planted in your life?
- What environment shaped your early understanding of God?
- Do you believe that seed is still alive inside of you?

Prayer

Lord, thank You for planting Your Word in my life, even when I didn't recognize it. Water it daily. Shine Your light on it. Let it grow and produce fruit in my life. Help me never to underestimate what You've already started. In Jesus' name, amen.

DAY 2

Jonah's Journey and Mine

Proverbs 3:5–6 - Trust in the LORD with all your heart, and do not lean on your own understanding. In all your ways acknowledge him, and he will make straight your paths.

Just like Jonah, I tried to run from my calling. I didn't want to face the purpose God had placed on my life. I thought I had it all figured out—how I'd live, where I'd go, what I'd do. But when you belong to God, He will let you go only so far before He calls you back.

I remember the moment it all started crashing. Everything I thought was stable began to fall. I was running from what God told me to do, and just like Jonah ended up in the belly of the whale and I found myself trapped. Not in a fish, but in a jail cell. That cell became my fish. My place of reflection. My place of redirection.

I couldn't see it at the time, but what felt like punishment was really God's grace. He was protecting me from myself. He was using isolation to wake me up and bring me back to purpose. Just like Jonah eventually went to Nineveh, I had to return to where I was called—to the Word, to the ministry, to helping others come out of their own belly experiences. And now, I don't run from the call. I run to it.

Scripture Focus

Jonah 1:3 - But Jonah rose to flee to Tarshish from the presence of the LORD. He went down to Joppa and found a ship going to Tarshish. So he paid the fare and went on board, to go with them to Tarshish, away from the presence of the LORD.

Reflection

When God calls you, you can either run with Him or run from Him. But even when you run, His love will chase you down. Jonah ran from the assignment because he didn't want to deal with what was uncomfortable. Many of us are the same. But God's call is not about comfort, it's about purpose. And He will meet you in your lowest place to restore that purpose.

Questions

- Have you ever felt like you were running from something God called you to?
- What "belly of the whale" moment has God used to get your attention?
- Are you ready to surrender to His plan for your life?

Prayer

Father, thank You for not giving up on me. Even when I tried to run, Your mercy followed me. Even when I tried to hide, Your purpose found me. Help me to stop resisting and start surrendering. Make me bold as Jonah after he repented. Let my life be a testimony of how You can still use those who once ran. In Jesus' name, amen.

DAY 3

Growing in the Storm

Psalm 1:3 - He is like a tree planted by streams of water that yields its fruit in its season, and its leaf does not wither. In all that he does, he prospers.

There was a season in my life when the storms just wouldn't stop. Trouble after trouble, trial after trial. I started wondering if I would ever catch a break. I felt like I was doing everything I could to stay grounded in God, but the winds just kept hitting me. It felt unfair. It was exhausting.

But then I started to notice something. Every time I got hit, I got stronger. Every time I was tested, I prayed more. Every time I lost something, I started depending more on what I couldn't lose, God's presence. That's when I realized that the storm wasn't sent to destroy me; it was sent to grow me.

Just like a tree needs water, wind, and even pressure to grow deep roots, I needed those seasons to build my foundation in Christ. It was in the worst weather that I saw the best fruit beginning to show in my life. Patience. Endurance. Humility. Prayer. I didn't like the process, but I couldn't deny the growth.

Scripture Focus

James 1:2–4 Count it all joy, my brothers, when you meet trials of various kinds, for you know that the testing of your faith produces steadfastness. And let steadfastness have its full effect, that you may be perfect and complete, lacking in nothing.

Reflection

God doesn't waste storms. If He allows it, He intends to use it. The same storm that shakes you is the storm that makes you. Don't rush out of the process. Stay planted. Let your roots grow deeper in God's Word. In due season, the fruit will show.

Questions

- What storm have you recently faced that God may be using to grow you?
- Can you recognize areas where you've grown stronger through past trials?
- How can you stay rooted when everything around you feels unstable?

Prayer

Lord, help me not to curse the storm but to trust the One who controls it. I know You are growing something in me, even when it hurts. Give me roots that run deep, faith that stands firm, and a heart that trusts Your process. Grow me until I look like You. In Jesus' name, amen.

DAY 4

God Is My Defender

Psalm 18:34–35 - He trains my hands for war, so that my arms can bend a bow of bronze. You have given me the shield of your salvation, and your right hand supported me, and your gentleness made me great.

While locked up in Norfolk, Virginia, facing 17 felony charges, I knew I had to lean on God like never before. I was far from home, carrying the weight of fear, pain, and confusion. But I didn't fold. I sought God. I stayed in prayer, woke up early for devotionals, and found strength in His presence.

Then a confrontation came. Another inmate attacked me. I hadn't gone looking for a fight, but when it came, God strengthened my hands like David. I stood my ground, but what happened after was even greater—the same man came back and apologized.

That moment showed me something deep: there's a time for peace, and there's a time for war. When God calls you to defend yourself, He equips you to do it without losing your integrity. The fight wasn't about violence—it became a testimony. God was, and still is, my Defender. He gives us discernment to know when to be still and when to stand.

Scripture Focus

Psalm 144:1 - Blessed be the LORD, my rock, who trains my hands for war, and my fingers for battle.

Reflection

Being a child of God doesn't mean we're always passive. There are moments when God will call us to stand firm. Like David, we may be outmatched in the natural, but God gives supernatural strength. What matters most is not the fight itself but how we fight. Do we walk in wisdom? Do we trust that God is still our defender, even in the battle?

Questions

- Have you ever had to physically or spiritually defend yourself?
- How do you balance humility with courage in conflict?
- Are you seeking God's wisdom in how and when to fight?

Prayer

Lord, thank You for being my strength and my defender. I know that You guide my steps and teach my hands when to fight and when to rest. Help me not to act in pride or fear, but with wisdom and courage. Let every battle I face bring You glory and draw others to Your peace. In Jesus' name, amen.

DAY 5

Church Is Not Walls—Church Is the Body

1 Corinthians 12:27 - Now you are the body of Christ and individually members of it.

When I first went to jail, I thought of church as a building—four walls, a pulpit, stained glass, and a choir. So when I looked around at the concrete, the bars, and the silence, it felt like a church was a million miles away. But as time went on, God began to show me something different.

It started small, with me reading my Bible and praying. Then men began asking me to pray for them, or to help them understand Scripture. Some just wanted encouragement, others were looking for answers they had never found before. The more this happened, the more I realized: *this is church.*

We didn't have pews, choirs, or microphones, but we had something better—people gathered in Jesus' name. Some were broken, some were searching, and some had no idea who they were in Christ. But as we came together, prayed together, and opened the Word together, God's presence met us. That cellblock turned into a sanctuary, not because of the space, but because of the Spirit of God working in His people.

God taught me that the Church isn't defined by walls, it's defined by people who believe in Him. The Church is His body, and when His people come together—whether in a building, in a house, or even in a jail—He is there.

Scripture Focus

1 Corinthians 12:27 - Now you are the body of Christ and individually members of it.

Reflection

Church is not a place you go; it's who you are as a believer in Christ. Too often we reduce it to a building or a Sunday service, but Scripture reminds us that *we are the body of Christ*. The power of the Church isn't in its walls but in its people—imperfect men and women transformed by God's **Spirit. Wherever believers gather in His name, the Church is alive and active.**

Questions

- Have you ever experienced "church" in an unexpected place?
- How does seeing the Church as people—not just buildings—change the way you live your faith?
- In what ways can you live out being part of the body of Christ this week?

Prayer

Lord, thank You for reminding me that the Church is not made of bricks and mortar, but of people who love You and follow You. Help me to live as a true member of Your body, serving, encouraging, and uplifting others wherever I am. Let my life be a witness that Your Church is alive in me. In Jesus' name, amen.

DAY 6

Praying in Elkhart Jail

Jeremiah 29:12 - Then you will call upon me and come and pray to me, and I will hear you.

When I was locked up in Elkhart Jail, I reached a crossroads. I could sit in despair and stay silent, or I could lift my voice to God. I chose to pray. At first, those prayers were quiet—just whispers between me and the Lord as I read my Bible.

But prayer has a way of stirring the atmosphere. Soon, other men started noticing. Some had never prayed before. Some had no background in church at all. Yet something pulled on their hearts. One by one, they asked me to pray for them. What began as a personal lifeline became a chain reaction.

Before long, we weren't just individuals surviving time in jail—we were brothers united in prayer. We stood in circles, hands joined, lifting our voices. There was no choir, no pastor, no service schedule—just raw faith. And the Spirit of God showed up.

That season taught me this: prayer is contagious. When one person is bold enough to call on God, others will follow. You never know who's watching, or whose heart is waiting for permission to seek Him too.

Scripture Focus

James 5:16 - Therefore, confess your sins to one another and pray for one another, that you may be healed. The prayer of a righteous person has great power as it is working.

Reflection

Prayer isn't just personal—it's powerful enough to shift an entire atmosphere. One person's obedience can spark faith in many. You may feel small or alone when you pray, but never underestimate how God can use your voice to ignite others.

Questions

- Do you see prayer as a personal duty or a contagious act that inspires others?
- Has your faith ever encouraged someone else to seek God?
- What atmosphere do your prayers create around you?

Prayer

Father, thank You for hearing every prayer I pray, no matter where I am. Teach me to call on You with boldness and to trust that You will respond. Use my prayers not only to strengthen me but to stir faith in others. Let revival start with me, right where I am. In Jesus' name, amen.

DAY 7

The Power of Fasting

Matthew 6:17–18 - But when you fast, anoint your head and wash your face, that your fasting may not be seen by others but by your Father who is in secret. And your Father who sees in secret will reward you.

I learned about fasting from my mother. I didn't understand it at first, but I saw her do it for years, especially when she was praying for my father's salvation. She would deny herself, press into the Spirit, and stay in the Word. Eventually, my father gave his life to Christ and became a believer. That stuck with me

Years later, I found myself in a place where I needed God to move, and move fast. I was in jail. I was broken. I needed answers. That's when I remembered how my mother sacrificed during fasting. However, that time, it wasn't just about not eating; it was about surrender. I fasted from food, but also from complaining, from fear, from doubt. And what I gained was so much more: clarity, peace, intimacy with God.

I fasted on house arrest too when no one could see. Fasting isn't about performance, it's about positioning. It's about removing the noise so you can hear clearly, and it works too. God met me every single time during my fasting periods.

Scripture Focus

Isaiah 58:6 - Is not this the fast that I choose: to loose the bonds of wickedness, to undo the straps of the yoke, to let the oppressed go free, and to break every yoke?

Reflection

Fasting is less about what you give up and more about what you gain. It realigns your heart with God. It empties you so He can fill you. When done with sincerity, it moves heaven. Don't underestimate what happens when you deny the flesh to seek the Spirit.

Questions

- Have you ever fasted with a spiritual purpose?
- What distractions might God be calling you to set aside?
- What area of your life needs clarity that only comes through seeking God more deeply?

Prayer

Father, help me to hunger more for You than for anything in this world. Teach me how to fast not for attention, but for alignment. Break every yoke in my life that keeps me bound. Strengthen my spirit when my flesh feels weak. Let my sacrifice bring me closer to You. In Jesus' name, amen.

DAY 8

Brothers in the Word

Proverbs 27:17 - Iron sharpens iron, and one man sharpens another.

While I was on house arrest, feeling isolated and overlooked, God sent me a lifeline—a community called *Brothers in the Word*. It wasn't a church building. It wasn't a formal program. It was a group of men coming together to grow in Christ.

I was invited by Pastor Sam, who I had originally met through marriage counseling. He connected me with a few others, including Pastor Tim. We met twice a week. We studied scripture, shared our struggles, and encouraged each other. Nobody was trying to impress or out-preach one another. We were just being real, and in that authenticity, God showed up.

For the first time in a long time, I saw the Church without walls. No offering plates. No judgment. Just brothers in the Word, sharpening each other. It helped restore my identity in Christ. It reminded me that I wasn't alone, and it gave me the boldness to start teaching others too.

Now, I'm not just a student, I'm a teacher in that same group. And it all started with one invitation and a yes to God.

Scripture Focus

Hebrews 10:24–25 - And let us consider how to stir up one another to love and good works, not neglecting to meet together, as is the habit of some, but encouraging one another, and all the more as you see the Day drawing near.

Reflection

God never meant for us to walk this journey alone. Community is where growth happens. Sometimes it won't look like a traditional church, but it will carry the heart of Jesus—truth, love, accountability, and support. Who are your brothers or sisters in the Word?

Questions

- Do you have a circle of believers that challenge and encourage you?
- How can you build or join a community that studies and lives out God's Word?
- What role might God be calling you to take within that circle?

Prayer

Lord, thank You for spiritual brothers and sisters. Thank You for placing people in my life who help me grow. Help me to be a faithful part of the body. Let me give as much as I receive. Use my voice, my testimony, and my time to sharpen someone else. Keep me rooted in Your Word and in godly community. In Jesus' name, amen.

DAY 9

Free in the Spirit, Though Bound in Chains

2 Corinthians 3:17 - Now the Lord is the Spirit, and where the Spirit of the Lord is, there is freedom.

There was a moment in jail when I looked around and realized something wild. I felt more free than I ever had outside those walls. How could that be? Because real freedom isn't physical. It's spiritual.

The more I got into God's Word, the more my mind was transformed. I stopped living by what I could see and started believing in what God said. I began worshipping and writing. I even found peace with other inmates who once wanted to fight me. The chains on my hands had nothing on the freedom in my soul.

When I left that place, I didn't just walk out a free man, I walked out a changed one. I walked out filled with purpose, filled with the Spirit, and unshackled in my identity. Being locked up taught me that liberty isn't about movement, it's about mindset. When you have Jesus, you're free wherever you are.

Scripture Focus

John 8:36 - So if the Son sets you free, you will be free indeed.

Reflection

True freedom isn't based on where you are, but Who is with you. The enemy wants you to think your environment determines your destiny. But God's Spirit brings liberty, no matter the setting. Are you walking in that freedom today?

Questions

- Have you ever felt free even when your situation looked limited?
- What does it mean to you to be free in the Spirit?
- How can you walk in that freedom every day, no matter your circumstances?

Prayer

Jesus, thank You for setting me free. Not just from physical chains, but from fear, doubt, and sin. Let me never forget that freedom is found in You. Teach me to live every day in the liberty of Your Spirit, no matter where I am. Make me a witness to others who still feel bound. In Jesus' name, amen

DAY 10

God's Mercy Speaks Louder Than Man's Judgment

Psalm 103:10 - He does not deal with us according to our sins, nor repay us according to our iniquities.

I once faced serious prison time over something as small as a candy wrapper. The police claimed my fingerprints tied me to a robbery. Because of my past, it was easy for them to assume I was guilty.

The truth? Yes, I had touched the wrapper—but I hadn't committed the crime. Still, that one detail and my record were used to build a case against me. I was placed on house arrest for 14 months. I couldn't work, I couldn't see my son, and I felt trapped. Yet even in that place, God was working.

I prayed. I gathered evidence. I asked God for favor. Eventually, my attorney was able to reduce the charges, and because I was a veteran, I was admitted into Veterans Treatment Court. When I graduated, every charge was dismissed. My record was wiped clean. That was nobody but God.

But he didn't stop there. Through Veterans Court, something else happened—something I had been trying to do for years. They helped me get my military discharge upgraded. This was something I had almost given up on, but God used this process to not only clear my name in the justice system, but also restore my honor in the military.

What the enemy meant for shame, God used for restoration. He showed me that His mercy runs deeper than man's judgment. He reminded me that my past doesn't disqualify me, because His grace is greater.

Scripture Focus

Lamentations 3:22–23 - The steadfast love of the LORD never ceases; his mercies never come to an end;they are new every morning; great is your faithfulness.

Reflection

False accusations and old labels can feel like chains, but God's mercy breaks them. People may judge you for who you used to be, but God sees you as redeemed. His mercy doesn't just spare you—it restores and clears your name. He not only brings you out, but He brings you up.

Questions

- Have you ever been wrongly accused or misunderstood?
- How has God's mercy restored things you thought were lost?
- In what ways can you trust Him to bring honor out of your shame?

Prayer

Father, thank You for being my Defender and my Restorer. Thank You for seeing past my mistakes and for covering me with mercy. Thank You for restoring things I had almost given up on. Help me to trust that what You have for me is greater than what anyone can take away. In Jesus' name, amen.

DAY 11

Feeding on the Right Things

Proverbs 4:22 - For they are life to those who find them, and healing to all their flesh.

When I was in prison in Indiana, I noticed something strange. So many men were joining gangs or following other religions just for survival or protection. It seemed like everyone was feeding on something—some kind of belief, system, or identity. God didn't allow me to go down that path. I chose to follow Christ.

But even though I thought I was different spiritually, physically I was still feeding on the same junk as everyone else—candy, snacks, and food with no nutritional value. Over time, it began to take a toll on my health. My blood sugar shot up so high that I was walking around as a diabetic without even knowing it. By the time the prison staff checked me, my numbers were over 600. The doctor told me that if I had fallen asleep that night without insulin, I may have never woken up.

That moment opened my eyes. God was showing me that just as junk food was destroying my body, feeding on the wrong spiritual food could destroy my soul. In a place full of false teachings and distractions, I had to be careful about what I allowed into my spirit. His Word became the only real food I could live on.

Now I see that both physically and spiritually, what you eat determines whether you live or die. Junk food makes the body weak, and false doctrine makes the soul weak. But God's Word is life—it nourishes, sustains, and heals.

Scripture Focus

Psalm 107:20 - He sent out his word and healed them, and delivered them from their destruction.

Reflection

God's Word is food for your soul. Just like your body can't survive off junk, your spirit can't survive off lies, fear, or empty philosophies. Every day, you're feeding on something—make sure it's His Word. That's where strength, truth, and real life are found.

Questions

- What "junk food" (spiritual or physical) have you been feeding on that leaves you weak?
- How has God's Word nourished you in seasons of struggle?
- What steps can you take to build a diet of Scripture into your daily life?

Prayer

Lord, thank You for teaching me that what I feed on matters. Protect me from the junk that weakens my body and the false teachings that starve my spirit. Help me to hunger for Your Word every day so that I may be strengthened, healed, and sustained. Make me mindful of what I consume, both physically and spiritually. In Jesus' name, amen.

DAY 12

Dreams and Deliverance

Job 33:15–16 - In a dream, in a vision of the night, when deep sleep falls on people, while they slumber on their beds, then he opens the ears of people and terrifies them with warnings.

While in jail, I had three dreams that still stay with me. They weren't just random occurrences either. They were prophetic, and every one of them came true.

In the first dream, I saw my mother across the street from me, but I couldn't get to her. Something like a dog had my leg. I woke up shaken. Soon after, my mother flew from Chicago to Virginia to be at one of my court dates, but I wasn't released. That dream became reality.

In the second dream, I was on the same side of the street as my mother. The same thing was holding me back, but I felt stronger. Shortly after that dream, the court began to lean more in my favor, but I was still not released.

The third dream showed me being completely free, walking down the street with nothing holding me. Sure enough, after years of struggle, God made a way. I was released. Not just physically, but spiritually. I knew the dreams were God's way of preparing and guiding me.

That experience taught me to pay attention when I sleep. God still speaks in the night, and sometimes, deliverance starts with a dream.

Scripture Focus

Genesis 41:25 - Then Joseph said to Pharaoh, "The dreams of Pharaoh are one; God has revealed to Pharaoh what he is about to do."

Reflection

God still speaks through dreams. Not every dream is from Him but some are divine instructions, warnings, or confirmations. If you're in a season of confusion, ask God to speak to you even in your sleep. Then write it down, and wait for Him to move.

Questions

- Has God ever spoken to you through a dream?
- Are you writing down what He shows you at night?
- How can you grow in discernment to know when a dream is from God?

Prayer

Father, thank You for speaking to me in ways I understand. Thank You for using dreams to guide and prepare me. Help me to be sensitive to Your voice, even while I sleep. Give me the wisdom to know what You are saying, and the faith to walk it out. Let every vision lead me closer to freedom. In Jesus' name, amen.

DAY 13

Stay Low to Stay Holy

James 4:10 - Humble yourselves before the Lord, and he will exalt you.

One day in prayer, I cried out to God with a trembling heart and these words: "Lord, help me to stay low. Let no pride be found in me." I saw what pride could do. How it can creep in even while you're doing good things, how it can ruin character, ruin purpose, and distance you from God.

At that moment, I wasn't asking for a position nor was I asking for recognition. I just wanted to stay close to His presence because I knew there is no life without Him.

That prayer became my posture whether I was teaching, fasting, writing, or simply leading my family. I wanted to stay low. I wanted my heart to reflect Jesus' humility, because I knew that the anointing only rests on surrendered ground.

Since then, I've made it a daily request: "Lord, strip me of pride. Keep me in Your will and help me to remember that the most powerful place I can be is on my knees."

Scripture Focus

Philippians 2:5–8 - Have this mind among yourselves, which is yours in Christ Jesus, who, though he was in the form of God, did not count equality with God a thing to be grasped, but emptied himself, by taking the form of a servant, being born in the likeness of men. And being found in human form, he humbled himself by becoming obedient to the point of death, even death on a cross.

Reflection

Pride is the enemy of power. God doesn't bless elevation if it costs you humility. Jesus was the Son of God and still He humbled Himself. If He had to stay low, so do we. Humility protects us, positions us, and keeps us under the covering of grace.

Questions

- In what areas of your life is God calling you to remain humble?
- How do you respond when pride tries to rise in your heart?
- What does it look like for you to "stay low" while living boldly in your faith?

Prayer

Lord, keep me low. Keep me surrendered. Keep me at Your feet where I belong. Help me to recognize pride and reject it. Let my character match my calling. Let me lead with humility, love with purity, and walk with You daily. I don't want anything that will pull me away from Your presence. Let my life be holy because it stays humble. In Jesus' name, amen.

DAY 14

A Second Chance to Love

Proverbs 17:17 - A friend loves at all times, and a brother is born for adversity.

When Myla, my wife, chose to stand by me, it wasn't easy for her. The world didn't make it easy. Friends who once loved her turned cold, and people who once encouraged her started whispering behind her back, all because of my past. The false charges painted me guilty in the eyes of people, even when they did not know the truth.

One of her closest friends went as far as to spread lies, straining our relationship and putting her in a place where she had to choose between approval and loyalty, but Myla stood. She stood in prayer. She stood in love. And most of all, she stood in faith.

She didn't just support me, she believed in what God was doing in me. When others walked away, her sister Bianca and her nieces remained. They were a representation of grace and real support. Through it all, I reminded Myla to pray for the others and not hold bitterness. The enemy can use even those closest to us to cause division.

Her unwavering love reminded me of God's faithfulness. When everyone else runs, God stays. Sometimes, He sends people like Myla to prove it.

Scripture Focus

Ruth 1:16 - But Ruth said, "Do not urge me to leave you or to return from following you. For where you go I will go, and where you lodge I will lodge. Your people shall be my people, and your God my God."

Reflection

Loyalty isn't proven in comfort, but it's revealed in conflict. When people talk, when lies spread, when storms hit, who stands with you? More importantly, who do you stand with? God honors covenant, and those who reflect His heart will love past people's opinions.

Questions

- Have you ever had to stand by someone when others walked away?
- How do you handle relationships when your faith is tested through them?
- Are you praying for those who may have hurt or misunderstood you?

Prayer

Lord, thank You for sending people who love like You. Thank You for Myla, for her courage and her loyalty. Help me to be someone who loves through the fire. Help me to forgive those who judge what they don't understand. Protect our hearts from bitterness. Let our relationships be rooted in prayer, patience, and perseverance. In Jesus' name, amen.

DAY 15

MYLA STANDS IN THE STORM

Proverbs 18:22 - He who finds a wife finds a good thing and obtains favor from the Lord.

After everything I had been through, including divorce, jail, and false accusations, I never thought I'd find love again. Truth be told, I wasn't even sure I deserved it. My heart had been wounded, and I didn't want to put anyone else through my pain. But God had other plans.

That plan was Myla. A woman full of grace, strength, and courage. She didn't meet me at my best; she met me in my brokenness. Instead of running, she prayed. Instead of doubting, she believed. She became a reflection of God's love to me. Not because life was perfect, but because our love was grounded in something greater than us—Jesus.

I remember looking at her and realizing that this wasn't just a relationship. It was redemption. God was showing me that He gives good gifts, even after we've messed up. He restores what was lost, and He uses love to do it. Real love. Not just emotion, but commitment, patience, and covenant.

Myla was and is my second chance. Every day I get to love her, I'm reminded that God's grace rewrites stories.

Scripture Focus

Joel 2:25 - I will restore to you the years that the swarming locust has eaten, the hopper, the destroyer, and the cutter, my great army that I sent among you.

Reflection

God is a Restorer. He doesn't just forgive, He rebuilds. Sometimes, He sends love as part of your healing. Don't let your past make you afraid of God's promises. If He says it's yours, trust Him to make it beautiful.

Questions

- Has God ever surprised you with a second chance?
- How can you honor those God sends into your life to walk with you?
- What past pain might God be using as preparation for restoration?

Prayer

Lord, thank You for second chances. Thank You for showing me that love can be holy, healing, and real. Help me never to take for granted the people You've placed in my life. Help me to love with patience, grace, and truth. Above all, may I keep You at the center of it all. In Jesus' name, amen.

DAY 16

Healed from False Accusations

Isaiah 54:17 - No weapon that is fashioned against you shall succeed, and you shall refute every tongue that rises against you in judgment. This is the heritage of the servants of the LORD, and their vindication is from me, declares the LORD.

There are few things more painful than being accused of something you didn't do. When lies are spoken against you, especially by people who once loved you, it cuts deep. That was my reality. False accusations tried to tear my life apart. They tried to break me, steal my voice, and rob me of the future God had promised.

But God.

He saw what no one else could. He knew the truth. But more than that, He defended me in ways I could never have done for myself. Even when I was on house arrest, isolated and misunderstood, He was working. He was clearing my name and healing my heart.

Those false accusations didn't destroy me, they drove me deeper into God's Word. They taught me how to trust His timing, not public opinion. Over time, the truth began to surface. The pain didn't disappear overnight, but God used it to shape my character and deepen my dependence on Him.

Now I walk in freedom, not just legally, but emotionally and spiritually. No lie can stick when God speaks the truth over your life.

Scripture Focus

Psalm 37:6 - He will bring forth your righteousness as the light, and your justice as the noonday.

Reflection

God is your vindicator. People may not always believe you, but He knows your heart. He promises that the truth will shine in time. So even when you're misunderstood, don't fight to prove yourself. Instead rest in the One who already knows and sees all.

Questions

- Have you ever been falsely accused or wrongly judged?
- How did you respond? How did God respond?
- What does it mean to let God be your defender instead of trying to clear your own name?

Prayer

Father, thank You for being my Defender. Thank You for knowing the truth when others believe a lie. Help me to trust You even when I'm falsely accused. Let me hold my peace and watch You fight for me. Heal my heart from every word that tried to break me. Restore what was lost and use my life to reflect Your righteousness. In Jesus' name, amen.

DAY 17

My Father's Grace and Forgiveness

Luke 15:20 - And he arose and came to his father. But while he was still a long way off, his father saw him and felt compassion, and ran and embraced him and kissed him.

For a long time, the relationship between my father and me was broken. There were things said, decisions made, and pain that stacked up between us. I didn't think we would ever fully understand each other again. However, when God started doing a work in me, He also began working on our relationship.

I remember the moment my father forgave me and welcomed me back into his life. I felt like the prodigal son returning home. There was no long lecture, just grace. He hugged me, and I could feel God's love through that embrace.

That moment reminded me that our Heavenly Father is the same waiting with open arms, ready to restore what's been broken. Now, I walk in that healing, knowing that grace makes room for relationship again.

Scripture Focus

2 Corinthians 5:18 - All this is from God, who through Christ reconciled us to himself and gave us the ministry of reconciliation.

Reflection

Forgiveness restores what pride ruins. Sometimes the hardest people to forgive are the ones closest to us, but God calls us to reconcile. Not just for them but for ourselves. Healing begins when humility walks in.

Questions

- Have you experienced reconciliation in a relationship you thought was over?
- What does it take to offer or receive grace in a difficult situation?
- How can you model the Father's love to someone who has hurt you?

Prayer

Lord, thank You for forgiving me even when I've failed You. Help me to extend that same grace to those around me. Heal every broken place in my relationships, and use me as a vessel of reconciliation. Let love speak louder than pride. In Jesus' name, amen.

DAY 18

No Life Without God's Presence

Psalm 51:11 - Do not cast me away from your presence, and do not take your Holy Spirit from me.

There came a moment when I realized I wasn't afraid of losing people, possessions, or positions, but I was afraid of losing God's presence. That's how serious it became for me. I told God, "You can take anything, just don't take Yourself from me."

I had learned what it felt like to live outside His presence, and nothing about it satisfied me. It left me empty, angry, confused. When His Spirit came close, everything shifted. I had peace in chaos, joy in pain, strength in weakness.

Now, I live with that fear, not in torment, but in reverence. I never want to be far from Him because outside of God, there is no life. And in Him, I have everything I need.

Scripture Focus

John 15:5 - I am the vine; you are the branches. Whoever abides in me and I in him he it is that bears much fruit, for apart from me you can do nothing.

Reflection

The presence of God is not a feeling, it's the foundation. Without Him, we drift. With Him, we thrive. Make it your priority every day to stay connected to His presence, no matter what it costs.

Questions

- Have you ever felt distant from God?
- What happens when you prioritize God's presence above everything else?
- How can you abide in Him daily?

Prayer

Father, I never want to live without You. Your presence is my peace, my strength, and my joy. Draw me closer every day. Let my heart stay sensitive to Your Spirit. May everything I do start and end with You. In Jesus' name, amen.

DAY 19

Rooted in the Word Through Trials

Colossians 2:7 - Rooted and built up in him and established in the faith, just as you were taught, abounding in thanksgiving.

Trials have a way of testing what you're really rooted in. I used to think I had strong faith until the storms came. That's when I learned the difference between knowing the Word and living by it.

When I was on house arrest, facing false charges, my emotions were unstable, but God's Word wasn't. I clung to scripture like it was food. The more I read it, the deeper my roots grew.

Now I know that trials don't come to break us; they come to bury the seed deep enough to grow strong. When you're rooted in the Word, no storm can uproot your faith.

Scripture Focus

Matthew 7:24–25 - Everyone then who hears these words of mine and does them will be like a wise man who built his house on the rock. And the rain fell, and the floods came, and the winds blew and beat on that house, yet it did not fall, because it had been founded on the rock.

Reflection

Being rooted in the Word isn't about memorizing verses. It's about trusting them. Storms reveal your foundation. Make sure yours is built on the Rock that cannot be shaken.

Questions

- What scriptures have kept you anchored during tough seasons?
- How are you cultivating deeper roots in God's Word?
- Is your faith built on truth or temporary emotions?

Prayer

Lord, let me be rooted in You. When storms come, let Your Word be my anchor. Teach me to not only hear, but to obey. Build my life on truth so I can stand strong in every season. In Jesus' name, amen.

DAY 20

Taste and See That the Lord Is Good

Psalm 34:8 - Oh, taste and see that the LORD is good! Blessed is the man who takes refuge in him.

I used to hear people say, "God is good," but I didn't fully believe it until I tasted that goodness for myself. It wasn't in the big moments; it was in the quiet ones. It was the times He gave me peace I didn't understand, favor I didn't earn, and grace I didn't deserve.

When I was fighting charges, sick in jail, and struggling with diabetes, it was the Word of God that nourished me. I remember fasting and saying to God, "I don't just want food, I want the meat of Your Word." And He gave it.

Now I teach others that you'll never know how good God is until you truly taste Him through obedience, prayer, surrender. Once you taste Him, everything else loses its flavor.

Scripture Focus

Jeremiah 15:16 - Your words were found, and I ate them, and your words became to me a joy and the delight of my heart, for I am called by your name, O LORD, God of hosts.

Reflection

God's goodness is best experienced, not explained. Taste His Word. Obey it. Let it fill you. Then watch it transform everything in you.

Questions

- What have you tasted that showed you God is truly good?
- Are you feeding your spirit or your flesh more often?
- How can you develop a stronger appetite for the Word?

Prayer

Lord, I want to taste Your goodness every day. Fill me with Your Word. Let it be sweeter than honey to my soul. Help me to hunger and thirst for righteousness. Let my life be evidence that You are good. In Jesus' name, amen.

DAY 21

Freedom in Surrender

Galatians 5:1 - For freedom Christ has set us free; stand firm therefore, and do not submit again to a yoke of slavery.

There's a powerful thing that happens when you finally give up control and give everything to God. I used to fight so hard to fix things myself. I thought I had to make everything right, prove my point, and carry the weight on my own shoulders. But that mindset only made me more broken.

It wasn't until I fully surrendered that I found true freedom. Not just freedom from jail, but freedom from bitterness, shame, and the pressure to be perfect.

When I let go, God stepped in. He rescued and transformed me. Surrender isn't weakness, it's where strength begins. Now I walk free. Not because I earned it, but because I laid it all down and let Him take over.

Scripture Focus

Romans 6:22 - But now that you have been set free from sin and have become slaves of God, the fruit you get leads to sanctification and its end, eternal life.

Reflection

True freedom starts at the altar of surrender. When you stop fighting and start trusting, God moves. Don't let pride or fear keep you bound. Give Him everything, and receive His peace in return.

Questions

- What areas of your life have you not fully surrendered to God?
- How has trying to control everything affected your peace?
- What does freedom look like for you today?

Prayer

Jesus, I surrender. I give You every part of me—my fears, my failures, and my future. Thank You for setting me free. Teach me to trust You more each day. Let my surrender be my strength, and my life bring You glory. In Jesus' name, amen.

DAY 22

When God Closed the Door

Revelation 3:7 - And to the angel of the church in Philadelphia write: 'The words of the holy one, the true one, who has the key of David, who opens and no one will shut, who shuts and no one opens.'

There were seasons where I thought God had abandoned me but He was just closing doors I didn't need to walk through. Doors I tried to force open in my own strength, but they led nowhere.

I was once trying to chase opportunities that looked good on the outside but weren't God's will. Every time a door shut, I felt rejection, but now I see it was protection. God didn't let me settle where He never planned for me to stay.

The closed doors led me to the right ones. They made me slow down, pray more, and listen for His voice. Each time I trusted Him, He opened something better, something lasting. If God closes a door, it's only because what's behind it isn't for you.

Scripture Focus

*Proverbs 3:6 - **In all your ways acknowledge him, and he will make straight your paths.***

Reflection

Closed doors aren't curses, but they're confirmations. They show that God is guiding you. Trust His *no* just as much as His *yes*. What He opens, no one can shut.

Questions

- What doors has God closed in your life that later made sense?
- Are you trying to force open something He already shut?
- How can you grow in trusting God's direction even when it's a no?

Prayer

Lord, thank You for every door You closed. Even when I didn't understand, You were protecting me. Help me to trust Your timing and Your direction. Teach me to wait, to listen, and to walk through only the doors You open. In Jesus' name, amen.

DAY 23

Victory Belongs to Obedience

Deuteronomy 28:1 - "And if you faithfully obey the voice of the LORD your God, being careful to do all his commandments that I command you today, the LORD your God will set you high above all the nations of the earth."

I used to think victory came from working harder or fighting louder. However, I've now learned that true victory comes through obedience. It's not about how much you do; it's about how closely you listen.

There were battles I lost because I moved before God told me to. Then there were battles I won simply because I obeyed. I recall being in situations where I wanted to react, defend myself, or make my own plans, but the Spirit said, "Wait."

When I listened, doors opened, peace came, and favor followed. Obedience is the key that unlocks divine victory. You don't need to be the strongest, you just need to be surrendered.

Scripture Focus

1 Samuel 15:22 - And Samuel said, "Has the LORD as great delight in burnt offerings and sacrifices, as in obeying the voice of the LORD? Behold, to obey is better than sacrifice, and to listen than the fat of rams."

Reflection

God honors obedience more than effort. If you want to win God's way, obey God's Word. Victory belongs to the ones who follow, not just the ones who fight.

Questions

- Have you ever seen God's favor follow a simple act of obedience?
- Are there any areas in your life where delayed obedience has held you back?
- How can you grow in listening for and following God's voice daily?

Prayer

Father, teach me to obey. Even when it's hard, even when it's inconvenient, help me to trust that Your way leads to victory. Silence every other voice but Yours. Let my heart respond to Your Word with faith and surrender. In Jesus' name, amen.

DAY 24

Your Weakness Is God's Opportunity

2 Corinthians 12:9 - But he said to me, "My grace is sufficient for you, for my power is made perfect in weakness." Therefore I will boast all the more gladly of my weaknesses, so that the power of Christ may rest upon me.

One of the most freeing truths I've learned is that I don't have to be strong all the time. God isn't looking for perfect people. He's looking for surrendered ones.

There were days in jail and on house arrest where I felt like I had nothing left. I was tired, unsure, and emotionally drained. But those were the very moments when God showed up the most. He spoke clearly. He comforted me deeply. He filled the gaps.

My weakness made room for His strength. I started to realize that my broken places were the best places for His glory to show up. Now I don't hide my weakness, but I use it as an invitation for God to be God.

Scripture Focus

Isaiah 40:29 - He gives power to the faint, and to him who has no might he increases strength.

Reflection

Weakness isn't a flaw—it's a doorway. When we admit our need, God responds with grace. Let Him shine through your struggle and show that His strength really is perfect.

Questions

- What areas of your life feel the weakest right now?
- How has God shown up in your lowest moments?
- Are you willing to let others see God's power through your story?

Prayer

God, I give You my weakness. I give You every place where I feel like I fall short. Let Your grace meet me there. Be strong where I can't be. Use my struggle to glorify Your name. In Jesus' name, amen.

DAY 25

Guard Your Heart in the Fire

Proverbs 4:23 - Keep your heart with all vigilance, for from it flow the springs of life.

One of the hardest battles I faced wasn't in the courtroom or the jail cell—it was in my own heart. When you've been betrayed, falsely accused, and isolated, bitterness tries to creep in. I had to learn how to guard my heart in the fire.

There were days I wanted to give in to anger, lash out, or shut down emotionally. Yet God kept calling me higher. He reminded me that a hardened heart can't be used and that healing begins in the heart.

So I started praying, not just for justice, but for joy. Not just for freedom, but for forgiveness. I was able to witness how God softened the hardest parts of me. I realized that guarding your heart isn't about closing it off. Rather it is a matter of keeping it clean.

Now, I don't just survive the fire, I worship in it because I've learned to protect the place where God speaks—my heart.

Scripture Focus

Ezekiel 36:26 - And I will give you a new heart, and a new spirit I will put within you. And I will remove the heart of stone from your flesh and give you a heart of flesh.

Reflection

Pain can either purify your heart or poison it. The difference is surrender. Let God filter your thoughts, your wounds, and your responses. A guarded heart is not blocked, it's healed, kept open to God for protection from offense.

Questions

- How do you typically respond when your heart is wounded?
- What does it look like to guard your heart without becoming cold?
- Are there areas of your heart that need healing or protection today?

Prayer

Father, help me guard my heart. Don't let pain harden me or bitterness take root. Keep me soft in Your hands and strong in Your Word. Heal every wound I carry and purify every motive in me. Let my heart reflect You, even in the fire. In Jesus' name, amen.

DAY 26

God is Still Writing My Story

Philippians 1:6 - And I am sure of this, that he who began a good work in you will bring it to completion at the day of Jesus Christ.

There were times in my life where I thought the story was over. The arrests. The accusations. The silence. I thought I had hit the last chapter, but God kept writing.

He wrote through the pain. Through the waiting. Through the days I doubted myself and questioned Him and every page turned into a new beginning. God reminded me that He's not done with my life, my purpose, or my calling.

Even now, I don't have all the answers. What I do have is a pen in the hand of a faithful Author. If He's still writing, then I'm still becoming. Don't close the book too soon for God's story for you is still unfolding.

Scripture Focus

Romans 8:28 - And we know that for those who love God all things work together for good, for those who are called according to his purpose.

Reflection

God is not finished with you. Your current chapter is not the conclusion. Trust Him to turn the page and keep writing beauty from ashes.

Questions

- Have you ever felt like your story was over before God said it was?
- How do you find hope in the middle of the unknown?
- What would it look like to trust God as your Author every day?

Prayer

Father, thank You for still writing my story. When I want to give up, remind me that You haven't. Write grace into my failures, purpose into my pain, and glory into every chapter. Let my life be a testimony to Your authorship. In Jesus' name, amen.

DAY 27

Purpose Over Popularity

Galatians 1:10 - For am I now seeking the approval of man, or of God? Or am I trying to please man? If I were still trying to please man, I would not be a servant of Christ.

One of the biggest temptations in life is chasing acceptance. I wanted people to like me, validate me, believe in me so God had to teach me that purpose will cost you popularity.

When I started walking in my calling, I lost people. When I stood for truth, I was misunderstood. Every loss became a gain in the Spirit. I learned that I didn't need applause; I needed alignment.

God's purpose doesn't always come with a crowd. Sometimes it comes with isolation. It's in that separation that He reveals your real identity. Now I choose calling over comfort, obedience over opinion, and destiny over likes.

Scripture Focus

Matthew 6:33 - But seek first the kingdom of God and his righteousness, and all these things will be added to you.

Reflection

You weren't called to be liked. You were called to be faithful. Don't trade your purpose for applause. God's reward is always greater than man's approval.

Questions

- Where have you felt pressure to please people more than God?
- How do you stay grounded in your calling when it's unpopular?
- What does it mean to choose purpose over popularity in your life?

Prayer

Lord, help me to seek You more than I seek applause. Teach me to value Your approval above all else. Let my life reflect Your calling, even if it costs me acceptance. Use me for Your glory, not my popularity. In Jesus' name, amen.

DAY 28

The Weight of Glory

2 Corinthians 4:17 - For this light momentary affliction is preparing for us an eternal weight of glory beyond all comparison.

There were seasons in my life where I felt the weight of affliction pressing on every side. Prison. Sickness. Loneliness. Betrayal. But God showed me that every trial had a purpose. What felt heavy was actually producing something eternal.

Through the pain, I found deeper worship. Through the struggle, I found unshakable faith. Through the isolation, I discovered the presence of God like never before.

Now I carry a new weight, which is the weight of glory. It's not a burden, but a calling. It's the anointing that came from the crushing. It's the story that gives hope to others still in the fire.

Scripture Focus

Romans 8:18 - For I consider that the sufferings of this present time are not worth comparing with the glory that is to be revealed to us.

Reflection

Glory is often birthed through pressure. What's heavy now will be holy later. Let the fire refine you not define you.

Questions

- What affliction has God used to reveal more of Himself to you?
- How has suffering shaped your faith?
- Are you carrying the weight of glory with humility and purpose?

Prayer

Jesus, thank You for using my pain to produce something greater. Help me not to waste my suffering. Let every trial refine me, every burden shape me, and every affliction prepare me for Your glory. In Jesus' name, amen.

DAY 29

Your Story Has Power

Revelation 12:11 - And they have conquered him by the blood of the Lamb and by the word of their testimony, for they loved not their lives even unto death.

For a long time, I was ashamed of my past. I didn't want to tell people what I had been through, what I had done or what had been done to me. God had to show me that my testimony wasn't a weakness, it was my weapon.

Every trial I survived became fuel for someone else's faith. Every tear I cried became a seed for someone else's healing. Every part of my story that once made me feel disqualified now gives God the glory. God didn't waste anything.

When I started sharing my story, I saw chains break in my life, and in the lives of others. Now I speak boldly because I know that the same story the enemy tried to use to shame me is the one God is using to set others free.

Scripture Focus

Psalm 107:2 - Let the redeemed of the LORD say so, whom he has redeemed from trouble (or "from the hand of the enemy").

Reflection

Your imperfect story has power because it proves God is faithful. Don't be silent about your deliverance. Someone needs to hear what God brought you through.

Questions

- Have you shared your testimony with someone who needed hope?
- What part of your story do you still feel afraid or ashamed to speak about?
- How can your testimony become a tool for healing and encouragement?

Prayer

Lord, thank You for redeeming every chapter of my story. Help me to speak with boldness, not fear. Use my testimony to reach those who are still in the struggle. Let my life declare Your victory. In Jesus' name, amen.

DAY 30

Isolation Was Preparation

Luke 5:16 - But he would withdraw to desolate places and pray.

At first, I saw isolation as punishment. Being separated from friends, family, and freedom felt like I was being forgotten. Over time, I realized God was not punishing me. He was preparing me.

In isolation, I found intimacy. I heard God more clearly. I read His Word with fresh eyes. He was pruning me, sharpening me, and revealing purpose that had been buried under pain and pride.

Now I look back and thank Him for the lonely places. What felt like a delay was actually a setup. He wasn't just preparing a place for me; He was preparing me for the place. Isolation birthed revelation.

Scripture Focus

Isaiah 30:15 - For thus said the Lord GOD, the Holy One of Israel, "In repentance and rest is your salvation, in quietness and trust is your strength,"

Reflection

Don't despise the quiet seasons. God does His best work in hidden places. What looks like a pause may be the preparation you've been praying for.

Questions

- How has God used isolation to get your attention?
- What lessons came from being in a place of stillness or separation?
- Are you ready for what He's been preparing you for?

Prayer

Father, thank You for using isolation to shape me. I now know that You weren't rejecting me, but refining me. Help me to value the quiet seasons and draw closer to You in them. Prepare me for what You've prepared for me. In Jesus' name, amen.

DAY 31

From Isolation to Population

Luke 15:24 - For this my son was dead, and is alive again; he was lost, and is found.' And they began to celebrate.

This is more than a book title, it's my life. I went from jail cells to pulpits, from isolation to community, from shame to purpose. God restored me and He revealed who I truly was.

Like the Prodigal Son, I came to myself in a distant place. I was tired, worn and done, but God welcomed me with open arms. He didn't just forgive me; He celebrated me. He clothed me, called me, and commissioned me.

Now I don't walk alone. I walk in purpose. I walk in family. I walk in population surrounded by those God has assigned to my journey. So, I declare this over you too: Your isolation was never the end. It was your invitation to discover identity, purpose, and power in Christ.

Scripture Focus

Jeremiah 29:11 - For I know the plans I have for you, declares the LORD, plans for welfare and not for evil, to give you a future and a hope.

Reflection

You were never meant to stay stuck. God uses isolation to unlock revelation. Let Him bring you into a new season of purpose, people, and population.

Questions

- What has God shown you about yourself during your time of isolation?
- How are you now walking in community and purpose?
- What would it look like to fully step into the population God prepared for you?

Prayer

God, thank You for bringing me out of isolation and into purpose. Thank You for restoring my life and filling it with people who reflect Your love. Use everything I've been through to help someone else walk in freedom. I declare that I'm no longer isolated. I'm walking in Your population. In Jesus' name, amen.

When I entered the military, I struggled to adapt to the authority that seemed more intent on breaking people down than building them up. Boot camp was not the place of brotherhood and encouragement I had imagined. Instead, it was harsh, dehumanizing at times. It was a hard lesson in how the world operates under the chains of human command. Yet even in the military structure, God showed me a glimpse of His kingdom. There is also a chain of command in His Kingdom but it is built on love, not fear.

During my time in service, I drifted from God. I didn't prioritize church, prayer, or reading my Bible. I was too busy chasing the life I thought was living — partying, drinking, using drugs, and living carelessly. Even then, God's hand was over me. He protected me when I didn't even know I needed protecting. Through jail cells, mental hospitals, and prisons, He stayed with me. Season after season, mistake after mistake, God was faithful.

Looking back, I don't regret the decisions I made. Even though I made the wrong choices, God's Word promises that He can make all things work together for good. He was writing my story even through my failures.

Being both a veteran and a felon is a heavy weight to carry in today's society. Veterans are often honored with words but forgotten in actions. Felons are often labeled as worthless, as if their lives no longer matter. Carrying both titles, I sometimes felt like society believed I should have never been born, but they are wrong.

When I raised my right hand and took an oath to serve my country, I did it by faith. I believed I was stepping into something greater. The same is true when I came to Christ. I believed by faith that Jesus was the Son of God who died and rose again to give me life. Faith is not the absence of trouble. It's the courage to keep going through it. Jesus Himself said, "In this life,

you will have trouble. But be of good cheer, for I have overcome the world."
(John 16:33)

Through the trials of being a veteran, a felon, and a child of God, I've learned that true faith is shown not when life is easy, but when patience, long-suffering, and perseverance are required. Every step I've taken, every season I've endured, has been by the grace of God. By that same grace, I moved from isolation to population, from brokenness to purpose and from survival to true life in Christ.

How to Unlock the Promises of God

Dear Reader,

As you finish this 31-day journey, I want to leave you with something even greater than my testimony: **the promises of God's Word.**

These promises are alive. They are not just verses to memorize ; they are truths to **live, pray, fast over,** and **believe** with your whole heart.

When I was walking through my darkest seasons, I didn't survive because of positive thinking. I survived because I **clung to God's Word.** I prayed it. I fasted while meditated on it.I repeated it back to God even when everything around me said otherwise.

God's Word is not magic, but it's **covenant**. In order to activate the promises and see them manifest in your life, here's what you need to do:

- **Pray the Word**: Speak these promises back to God. Thank Him in advance for them.
- **Meditate on the Word**: Read them slowly. Think about them day and night.

- **Fast and Focus**: Sacrifice distractions and fleshly desires so you can hear God more clearly.
- **Wait and Trust**: God's timing is not your timing. Waiting strengthens your faith.
- **Stay Connected to the Vine**: Stay close to Jesus. He is the Source of life and growth.
- **Be Patient with the Process**: Growth doesn't happen overnight. Trust the shaping.

Remember: *The seed is planted when you hear the Word. The watering comes through prayer, fasting, and obedience. The harvest comes in God's perfect timing.*

You are not forgotten. You are not abandoned. **You are being prepared.**

Stay low, stay hungry, stay faithful. The promises are real and they are for you.

30 Promises of God for the Isolated Heart

(Meditate, pray, and believe these daily!)

1. **Deuteronomy 31:6** — God will never leave nor forsake you.
2. **Isaiah 41:10** — Fear not, for He is with you.
3. **Joshua 1:9** — Be strong and courageous, the Lord your God is with you.
4. **Psalm 23:4** — Even in the valley, He is with you.
5. **Romans 8:38-39** — Nothing can separate you from His love.
6. **2 Timothy 1:7** — You have power, love, and a sound mind.
7. **John 8:36** — Who the Son sets free is free indeed.

8. **Philippians 1:6** — He who began a good work in you will complete it.
9. **Psalm 34:18** — The Lord is close to the brokenhearted.
10. **Isaiah 43:2** — When you pass through the waters, He will be with you.
11. **Matthew 5:4** — Blessed are those who mourn, for they shall be comforted.
12. **James 4:8** — Draw near to God and He will draw near to you.
13. **Romans 8:1** — There is no condemnation for those in Christ Jesus.
14. **1 Peter 5:7** — Cast all your cares on Him because He cares for you.
15. **2 Corinthians 4:8-9** — You are hard-pressed but not crushed.
16. **Jeremiah 29:11** — His plans for you are good, for a future and a hope.
17. **Hebrews 13:5-6** — The Lord is your helper; you will not be afraid.
18. **Psalm 91:1-2** — You dwell under the shadow of the Almighty.
19. **John 14:27** — His peace He leaves with you.
20. **Psalm 121:7-8** — The Lord will keep you from all harm.
21. **Romans 5:8** — Christ died for you while you were still a sinner.
22. **2 Corinthians 5:17** — You are a new creation in Christ.
23. **Psalm 27:10** — Even if others forsake you, the Lord will receive you.
24. **Matthew 28:20** — Jesus is with you always, to the very end.
25. **Isaiah 26:3** — He keeps you in perfect peace when your mind is stayed on Him.
26. **Psalm 30:5** — Weeping may endure for a night, but joy comes in the morning.
27. **Philippians 4:19** — God will supply all your needs.
28. **1 Peter 2:9** — You are a chosen generation, a royal priesthood.
29. **Colossians 3:3** — Your life is hidden with Christ in God.
30. **Revelation 21:4** — He will wipe away every tear.

Preview of *Soldier to Son*

Testimony:

I'll never forget stepping into basic training. It was like being dropped into

another world—a world where nothing was about you anymore. No one cared where you came from, what you believed, or what kind of man you thought you were. The goal was simple: break you down, then build you back up.

In those early weeks, everything I relied on–my confidence, my opinions, and my independence was tested. My pride was challenged every day. I was sleep-deprived, pushed to physical limits, yelled at, and forced to conform to a structure bigger than myself. It wasn't just about drills and formations. It was about surrendering who I was to become who they needed me to be.

But little did I know, God was using that very system to begin His own breaking process in me. It was preparation for something deeper than military discipline. He was stripping me spiritually, not just physically. In that moment, I didn't know I was being shaped—not just into a soldier, but into a vessel for the Kingdom.

Spiritual Insight:

Just like the military breaks a man to train him, God breaks us to rebuild us in His image. He breaks the pride that says, "I've got this." He breaks the fear that whispers, "You'll never change." He breaks the self-reliance that tries to solve everything without Him. And in that breaking, He's not destroying you; He's delivering you.

It's in the breaking where the real training begins. God doesn't train sons through comfort; He trains them through surrender. What basic training was for my body, brokenness was for my spirit. It was in that humbled place I could finally hear His voice and learn how to walk with Him.

Coming in 2026

About the Author

Eric Devon Jefferson Jr. was born and raised on the south side of Chicago, where faith and survival intertwined daily. At an early age, the seeds of Christ were planted at Apostolic Faith Church under Bishop Dr. Horace E. Smith. But like many, Eric's journey led him through storms, seasons of rebellion, military service, incarceration, heartbreak, and loss.

Growing up, Eric once thought that being saved or knowing God wasn't cool, but he later realized that knowing God at an early age was the very thing that rescued him as an adult. It was in his trials and seasons of isolation that the seed planted in childhood began to bloom. He thanks God for the Sunday School classes his grandmother took him to at Apostolic Faith Church, and the prayers his mother lifted early each morning before work.

Eric also honors the men of God who poured into him throughout his journey, helping him grow into the man he is today. Now a husband and father of four children, Eric is the founder of One-Way Ministry, a faith-based initiative dedicated to reaching those who feel isolated, forgotten, and broken. He is passionate about helping people discover their identity in Christ and empowering them to walk boldly in purpose.

Eric's life is a living testimony that God redeems, restores, and revives. He is forever grateful for every experience God allowed him to grow through and hopes this book inspires others to find God in their own wilderness.

www.ingramcontent.com/pod-product-compliance
Lightning Source LLC
Chambersburg PA
CBHW031421160426
43196CB00008B/1011